SMART MONEY

"saving and investing for kids"

S. Deep Perera

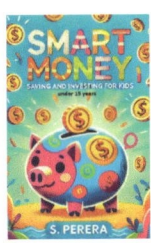

For my three incredible sons,

You are my heart, my pride, and my purpose. More than life itself, I love each of you. May you grow up with the wisdom to use money as a tool for good, to dream big, and to never forget that true wealth is found in kindness, curiosity, and courage. This book is for you, as you embark on your own journeys to build bright, purposeful futures.

With all my love and hope, always.

CONTENTS

Title Page
Dedication
Introduction : Let's Learn About Money!   1
Chapter 1 : What is Money?   3
Chapter 2 : Where Does Money Come From?   6
Chapter 3 : Why Should We Save Money?   8
Chapter 4 : Different Ways to Save   11
Chapter 5 : Spending Wisely   15
Chapter 6 : How to Make Your Savings Grow   18
Chapter 7 : Types of Investments   21
Chapter 8 : Starting Your Own Business   25
Chapter 9 : Giving Back   27
Chapter 10 : Building Good Money Habits   29
Chapter 11 : Making Money Decisions   31
Chapter 12 : How to Handle Money Mistakes   34
Chapter 13 : Setting Money Goals   37
Chapter 14 : How Money Can Help Others   40
Chapter 15 : Future Money Goals   43
Chapter 16 : Fun Money Challenges!   45
Chapter 17 : Money Quizzes and Puzzles   48
Chapter 18 : Create Your Own Money Plan   50

chapter :19 Let's Talk About Money in the Future	51
Chapter 20 : You're a Money Expert Now!	53
Afterword	57
About The Author	59

INTRODUCTION: LET'S LEARN ABOUT MONEY!

Hi there! Welcome to the world of **smart money**. Have you ever wanted to buy something cool, like a toy, video game, or even a new pair of shoes? You probably already know that you need money to do that, right? But do you know how to **save** money and make it **grow** over time?

This book will teach you how to:
- **Save money** for the things you want.
- **Spend wisely** so you can buy what you need and still have money left.
- **Invest** little by little to grow your savings like a tree grows from a seed!

By the end of this book, you'll be a **Money Boss**—someone who knows how to handle money like a pro. Ready? Let's dive in and start learning!

CHAPTER 1 : WHAT IS MONEY?

You've probably heard people say, "I need money to buy this," or "That costs a lot of money!" But what exactly **is** money, and why do we need it?

What is Money?

Money is something we use to buy things we want or need, like toys, food, or clothes. A long time ago, people didn't have money. Instead, they traded things. If someone wanted bread, they'd give the baker something in exchange, like eggs or milk. This was called **bartering**. But bartering was hard because not everyone wanted the same things. That's when money was invented!

Money comes in many forms:

- **Coins**: Small, shiny metal pieces.
- **Bills**: Paper money like dollar bills.
- **Digital Money**: Money you can't touch but use through a card or app (like when you swipe your debit card at the store).

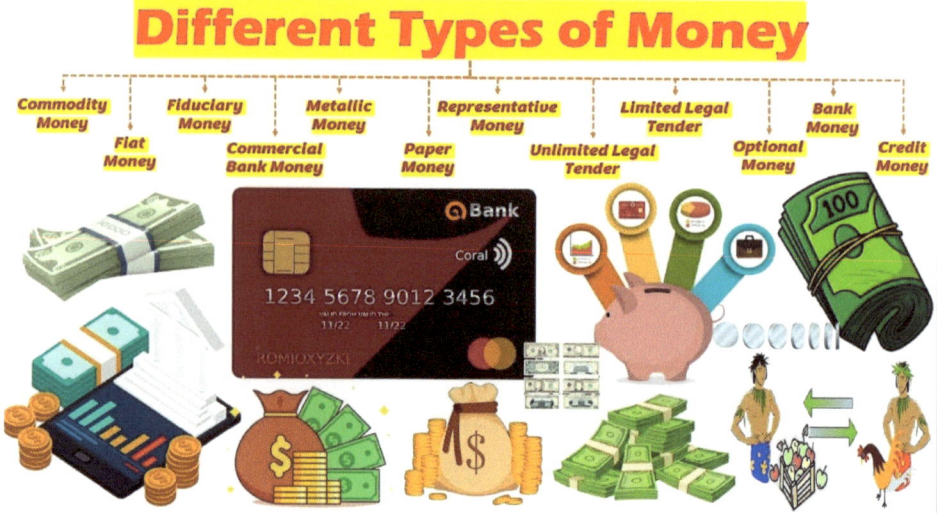

Where Do We Keep Money?

Most people keep their money in a **bank**. The bank helps keep it safe. You can save your money there and even earn a little bit of extra money called **interest**!

Money All Around the World

Did you know that every country has its own type of money? In the U.S., we use **dollars**. In Japan, they use **yen**. In Europe, they use **euros**. No matter what type of money it is, people use it to buy things everywhere!

Activity: Design Your Own Money!

What would your own money look like if you could create it? Draw a picture of your own coin or bill. What color would it be? Whose picture would be on it?

SMART MONEY

CHAPTER 2 : WHERE DOES MONEY COME FROM?

So, now that you know what money is, where does it come from? Do you just magically get it when you need it? Not exactly. You need to **earn** money by doing work or getting it as a gift.

Earning Money

There are lots of ways you can earn money, even as a kid! You might:

- Get an **allowance** from your parents for doing chores around the house.

- Help your neighbors with small jobs, like walking their dog or raking leaves.
- Earn money for good grades or special achievements.
- Get money as a gift from your family on your birthday or during the holidays.

Every dollar you earn is like a little piece of **power**—it gives you the ability to buy what you want or save for something special.

Activity: List Your Money Jobs!

Think about all the ways you can earn money. Make a list of the chores or jobs you can do at home or in your neighborhood. Write them down and decide how much you want to save from each one.

-
-
-
-
-
-

CHAPTER 3 : WHY SHOULD WE SAVE MONEY?

Now that you know how to earn money, you might want to spend it right away. But wait! Saving money is super important. Why? Because saving money helps you buy bigger and better things in the future.

What is Saving?

Saving money means putting some of it aside instead of spending it all at once. It's like keeping it safe for later. Think of saving like a game: the more you save, the closer you get to buying something you really want.

Why Save?

Here's an example: Let's say you really want a new bike, and it costs $100. But right now, you only have $20. Instead of spending that

$20 on smaller things, you can put it in a **savings jar** or a **bank account**. Each time you earn more money, you add to your savings until you have enough to buy the bike!

Saving helps us:
- Buy **big things** we really want.
- Have **emergency money** for when something unexpected happens.
- **Feel secure** knowing we have extra money for the future.

Activity: Set a Savings Goal!

What's something you really want? Is it a toy, a game, or maybe a new pair of shoes? Write down how much it costs and how much money you need to save to get there. Set a goal for yourself and track how close you are to reaching it!

• $

CHAPTER 4 : DIFFERENT WAYS TO SAVE

Now that you know **why** you should save, let's explore the different ways you can actually **do** it! There are a few fun and easy ways to keep your money safe until you're ready to spend it on something awesome.

Saving in a Piggy Bank

The most common way to save money when you're a kid is using a **piggy bank**. Have you seen one before? It's a little container shaped like a pig (or sometimes other animals), and you can drop your coins and bills inside. When it's full, you can open it up and see how much money you've saved!

Opening a Savings Account

SMART MONEY

When you're ready to level up your savings game, you can open a **savings account** at a bank. A savings account is like a **super secure** piggy bank that earns you extra money, called **interest**. It's perfect if you want to save for something big, like a bike or a special vacation.

Here's how it works:

1. You put your money in the account.
2. The bank keeps it safe.
3. Over time, the bank gives you a little bit of extra money (interest) just for keeping it there!

Digital Savings

In the digital age, you can also use apps to track your savings. These apps work like virtual piggy banks. Some apps even let you set savings goals and remind you to save each week!

But remember, no matter where you save, the important thing is to **keep saving** little by little!

Activity: Design Your Own Piggy Bank!

If you could make a piggy bank shaped like anything, what would it be? Draw a picture of your dream piggy bank. Would it be a cat, a dinosaur, or maybe even a rocket?

CHAPTER 5 : SPENDING WISELY

Now that you've learned how to save, let's talk about **spending**. Spending money is fun, but if you're not careful, you might spend it all at once and have nothing left for later! This is why it's important to learn how to **spend wisely**.

Needs vs. Wants

One of the biggest lessons about money is learning the difference between a **need** and a **want**. A **need** is something you can't live without, like food, clothes, or a place to live. A **want** is something fun but not necessary, like candy or video games.

Here's a simple way to think about it:

- **Needs**: Things you must have.
- **Wants**: Things that are nice to have.

When you learn to save for your **wants** after taking care of your **needs**, you become a **Money Boss**!

Budgeting Basics

A **budget** is like a map for your money. It helps you decide how much to save, how much to spend, and even how much to give to others. Here's a simple budget you can follow with your allowance or money you earn:

    1. **Save** 50% of your money.
    2. **Spend** 40% on fun stuff (wants).
    3. **Give** 10% to help others (charity).

Let's say you get $10 as an allowance. Here's what you could do:

- Save $5 for something big, like a toy.
- Spend $4 on something fun, like a treat or a small toy.
- Give $1 to charity or help someone in need.

Activity: Make Your Own Mini-Budget!

Take the money you earn or get as a gift this week. Make a mini-budget for it, using the 50/40/10 rule. Write down how much you want to save, spend, and give!

CHAPTER 6 : HOW TO MAKE YOUR SAVINGS GROW

Did you know your money can grow without you doing much at all? It's called **investing**! When you invest, you put your money in places where it can grow over time. It's like planting a seed in the ground and watching it turn into a big tree with lots of fruit.

What is Investing?

Investing means using your money to buy things that will make you **more** money over time. For example, when adults buy **stocks**, they're buying a small part of a company. If the company does well, they can make extra money!

Here's a fun way to think about it:

- **Saving** is like putting your money in a piggy bank.
- **Investing** is like planting a money seed that grows into a money tree!

Starting Small

You don't need a lot of money to start investing. Even if you only have a little, you can invest and watch your money grow over time. The secret is to be patient!

How Interest Works

Interest is like a reward from the bank for saving your money. Let's say you put $100 in a savings account. Every year, the bank will give you a little extra (maybe $5) just for keeping your money there. That's interest!

Activity: Watch Your Money Grow!

Imagine you put $100 in a savings account that gives you $5 in interest every year. After 1 year, you'd have $105. After 2 years, you'd have $110. How much would you have after 5 years? (Hint: Keep adding $5 each year!)

CHAPTER 7 : TYPES OF INVESTMENTS

Now that you know what **investing** is, let's look at some different types of investments you can try. Don't worry—you don't need a lot of money to start, and you don't need to be an expert. Even kids can begin investing with a little help from adults!

Simple Investments

A simple way to start investing is with something safe, like a **savings account** or **bonds**. When you invest in bonds, you're lending your money to the government or a company, and they promise to pay you back with a little extra (interest).

- **Savings Account**: Safe place to store your money and earn a little interest.
- **Bonds**: Another safe way to lend money and earn interest over time.

What are Stocks?

Stocks are a little more exciting! When you buy a **stock**, you're buying a tiny piece of a company. That means if the company does well, your stock becomes more valuable, and you can make money. But if the company doesn't do well, you might lose some money too. That's why stocks can be a little risky, but they can also be fun and rewarding!

The Magic of Compound Interest

Compound interest is one of the most powerful ways to make your savings grow. It means you earn interest not only on the money you save but also on the interest you've already earned! It's like a snowball rolling down a hill, getting bigger and bigger.

Let's say you save $100 and earn $5 in interest. Next year, you earn interest not just on your original $100, but on $105! This way, your money keeps growing faster and faster.

Activity: Watch the Snowball Effect!

Imagine you start with $100 and earn 5% interest every year. After the first year, you'll have $105. After the second year, you'll have $110.25. How much will you have after 5 years? (Hint: Use a calculator and multiply by 1.05 each year!)

CHAPTER 8 : STARTING YOUR OWN BUSINESS

Did you know that you can **earn money** by starting your own small business? You don't need to be an adult to be a business owner! Lots of kids start small businesses to earn extra money, and it can be really fun.

Small Business Ideas for Kids

Here are some business ideas you can try:

- **Lemonade Stand**: Sell refreshing lemonade to your neighbors on a hot day.
- **Dog Walking**: Offer to walk dogs in your neighborhood for a small fee.
- **Lawn Mowing**: Help your neighbors by mowing their lawns and earning money.

- **Craft Sales**: Make and sell your own crafts, like friendship bracelets or painted rocks.

How to Save and Invest Profits

When you start earning money from your small business, don't forget to save some of it! You can use the same **50/40/10 rule**:

- **Save** 50% for something big.
- **Spend** 40% on fun stuff.
- **Give** 10% to charity.

Activity: Design Your Own Business Sign!

If you were to start a business, what would you sell? Design a fun and creative sign for your business. Would you sell lemonade, crafts, or maybe something else?

CHAPTER 9 : **GIVING BACK**

One of the most rewarding things you can do with your money is **give back** to others. Giving helps people in need and makes the world a better place. Plus, it feels good to help!

Why Giving is Important

When you give to a cause you care about, you're making a difference in someone's life. You could donate money to help the environment, support animal shelters, or give to a charity that helps kids in need.

How Much Should You Give?

You don't have to give a lot—even a small amount can make a big difference. If you follow the **50/40/10 rule**, you'll set aside 10% of your money for giving. That means if you earn $10, you can give $1 to a cause you care about.

Activity: List Causes You Care About!

Think about what's important to you. Do you love animals? Do you want to help kids who don't have enough food? Make a list of causes that are close to your heart, and decide how much you'd like to give to each one.

CHAPTER 10 : BUILDING GOOD MONEY HABITS

Good money habits are the key to becoming a **Money Boss**. These are simple things you can do every day to make sure you're saving, spending wisely, and planning for the future.

Money Habits for Life

Here are some habits that will help you manage your money like a pro:

- **Save regularly**: Try to save a little bit every week, even if it's just a few dollars.
- **Track your spending**: Write down what you spend your money on, so you can see where it goes.
- **Invest wisely**: When you're ready, invest your money to help it grow over time.

Keeping Track of Your Money

One way to stay on top of your money is by keeping a **money journal**. You can write down how much you've saved, what you've spent, and how much you've earned. This way, you'll always know how much money you have!

Activity: Make a Savings Tracker!

Create your own savings tracker. Draw a picture of a thermometer, and as you save more money, color in the thermometer to see how close you are to reaching your goal!

CHAPTER 11 : MAKING MONEY DECISIONS

Now that you know how to save, invest, and even give money, it's time to learn how to make smart money decisions. Every time you spend or save money, you're making a decision. Sometimes it's hard to know the best choice, but with a few tips, you can make the right decision every time!

The Power of Patience

One of the best money decisions you can make is learning to be **patient**. When you see something you want, it's easy to spend your money right away. But waiting a little bit might help you make a better choice. Patience is like a superpower that helps you save for bigger, better things.

Needs First, Wants Later

Another smart money decision is to always take care of your **needs** first. If you spend all your money on wants, you might not have enough for the things you really need. Make a habit of asking yourself, "Do I need this or do I just want it?"

Creating a Decision Checklist

Here's a simple checklist to help you decide whether to spend or save:

     1. Do I need this right now?
     2. Is this something I can save for later?
     3. Will I still want this in a week or a month?
     4. Do I have enough money saved for something bigger?

If you answer "yes" to most of these questions, you're ready to make a smart money decision!

Activity: Practice Decision Making!

Think of something you want to buy right now. Go through the decision checklist and see if you should buy it now or wait and save for something bigger.

CHAPTER 12 : HOW TO HANDLE MONEY MISTAKES

Nobody's perfect, and sometimes we make mistakes with money. Maybe you spent all your money on candy and didn't have enough left for a new game. That's okay! What's important is learning from your mistakes so you don't make the same one again.

What is a Money Mistake?

A money mistake is when you spend your money in a way you didn't plan, and then you don't have enough for something important. The good news is that everyone makes mistakes with money, even adults!

Learning from Your Mistakes

The best way to handle a money mistake is to learn from it. Ask yourself:

- What did I spend my money on?
- How did it feel to not have enough for something important?
- What will I do differently next time?

Once you know the answers, you can make better money choices in the future.

The Bounce-Back Plan

If you make a mistake with money, here's how to bounce back:

1. **Save** a little extra next time.
2. **Plan** what you'll spend your money on before you buy anything.
3. **Be patient** and remember that everyone makes mistakes.

Activity: Money Mistake Detective!

Think about a time you made a money mistake. Write down what you spent your money on and how you could have spent or saved it differently.

CHAPTER 13 : SETTING MONEY GOALS

A **money goal** is something you plan to buy or achieve with your money. Setting goals is important because it gives you something to work toward. Whether it's saving for a new video game, a bike, or even college, having a goal helps you stay focused.

What's a Money Goal?

A money goal is something specific that you want to do with your money. It could be buying something, saving a certain amount, or giving money to a charity. Your goal should be:

- **Specific**: Know exactly what you're saving for.
- **Measurable**: Know how much you need.
- **Achievable**: Make sure it's something you can actually reach.

Short-Term vs. Long-Term Goals

There are two types of money goals:

- **Short-term goals**: Things you want to buy soon, like a toy or a book.
- **Long-term goals**: Things you save for over a long time, like a bike or a computer.

How to Set a Goal

Here's how you can set a money goal:

1. Write down what you want.
2. Write down how much it costs.
3. Decide how long it will take to save.
4. Start saving!

Activity: Set Your Own Money Goal!

Think about something you want to save for. Write down what it is, how much it costs, and how long it will take to save. Make a plan for reaching your goal.

CHAPTER 14 : HOW MONEY CAN HELP OTHERS

We've talked about how money can help you, but did you know it can also help other people? When you give money to charity or help someone in need, you're making a difference in their lives. Helping others with your money is one of the best things you can do.

What is Charity?

Charity is when you give money, time, or things to people who need help. You might give money to a homeless shelter, donate toys to kids in need, or help your local animal shelter.

Why Giving Feels Good

When you help others, it makes you feel good inside. Knowing that you've made someone else's day better is one of the best feelings in the world.

How Much Should You Give?

You don't need to give a lot—even a small amount can make a big difference. If you save part of your allowance for charity, you'll always have a little bit to give to those who need it.

Activity: Plan a Giving Goal!

Choose a cause that's important to you, like helping animals, protecting the environment, or feeding hungry people. Set a goal for how much you want to give and write down how you'll reach that goal.

CHAPTER 15 : FUTURE MONEY GOALS

Even though you're a kid now, it's never too early to start thinking about the future. Maybe one day you'll want to go to college, buy a car, or even start your own business. Setting goals for the future will help you make your dreams come true.

Big Dreams, Big Goals

Think about your future. What do you want to do when you grow up? Do you want to travel the world, buy a house, or start a company? No matter what your dream is, you'll need to save and invest money to make it happen.

How to Save for the Future

Here's how you can start saving for the future right now:

1. **Set a long-term goal**: What do you want in the future?
2. **Start small**: Even saving a few dollars now can make a big difference later.
3. **Be patient**: It might take a while, but saving little by little adds up.

Activity: Write a Letter to Your Future Self!

Write a letter to your future self about what you want to do with your money. Will you save for college, a car, or something else? Seal the letter and open it in a few years to see if you're on track!

CHAPTER 16 : **FUN MONEY CHALLENGES!**

Are you ready to become a **Money Master**? Let's put your skills to the test with some fun money challenges! These activities will help you practice saving, spending, and making smart money decisions. Plus, they're super fun to do with friends and family.

Challenge 1: The One-Week No-Spend Challenge

For one whole week, try not to spend any of your money! That means no candy, toys, or games—just saving every penny. See if you can make it through the week without spending anything.

Challenge 2: The $10 Savings Goal

Grab $10 (or another amount you want to start with) and try to save it as fast as possible! You can save your allowance, do small jobs, or even sell something you no longer need. The goal is to reach $10 in savings by the end of the week.

Challenge 3: The Family Spending Freeze

Get your whole family involved! For one day, challenge your family not to spend any money. No take-out, no shopping, nothing. See if you can all make it through the day without spending a single dollar.

Challenge 4: The Savings Jar Race

This one's super fun! Get an empty jar and decorate it with your name. Then, challenge your family or friends to a **savings race**. Whoever fills their jar with the most money in one month wins a fun prize—like picking the next family movie night!

CHAPTER 17 : MONEY QUIZZES AND PUZZLES

Now it's time to test your money knowledge! See how much you've learned about saving, spending, and investing by trying these fun quizzes and puzzles. Don't worry if you don't know all the answers—you can always go back and read the chapters again!

Quiz 1: True or False

1. You should spend all your money as soon as you get it. (False)
2. You can invest by buying a piece of a company called a stock. (True)
3. Patience is important when saving money. (True)
4. It's impossible for kids to start a business. (False)
5. Saving and investing are the same thing. (False)

Quiz 2: Which is the Best Choice?

1. You want to buy a new video game, but you don't have enough money yet. Do you:
   - A. Spend your money on candy instead.
   - B. Save a little each week until you have enough for the game.
   - C. Ask your friend to buy it for you.
2. You've earned $20 from doing chores. What should you do with it?
   - A. Spend all of it on toys right away.
   - B. Save some of it and spend a little on something fun.

- C. Hide it under your bed.

Puzzle Time: Word Search

Find these money words hidden in the grid:

- **Save**
- **Invest**
- **Spend**
- **Goal**
- **Interest**
- **Budget**

CHAPTER 18 : CREATE YOUR OWN MONEY PLAN

Now that you've learned all about saving and investing, it's time to create your own money plan! A money plan helps you figure out how much you want to save, what you'll spend, and how you'll reach your goals.

Step 1: Write Down Your Goals

Start by thinking about what you want to save for. Is it a new bike? A fun trip? Write down your top 3 money goals.

Step 2: Plan Your Spending

Next, think about how much you want to spend each week. Remember the **50/40/10 rule**:

- Save 50% of your money.
- Spend 40% on fun stuff.
- Give 10% to charity or those in need.

Activity: Make a Money Plan!

Use this simple template to make your own money plan:

- **Money Goal**: (What are you saving for?)
- **How Much I'll Save Each Week**: (How much can you save?)
- **What I'll Spend On**: (What fun things will you spend your money on?)
- **How I'll Help Others**: (What cause will you give to?)

CHAPTER :19 LET'S TALK ABOUT MONEY IN THE FUTURE

What will money be like when you're all grown up? Who knows! There might be new types of money or different ways to save and invest. But one thing will always stay the same—**smart money habits** will help you reach your dreams, no matter what the future holds.

Digital Money

Have you heard of digital money, like **Bitcoin** or **online wallets**? These are new ways people are using money today. Instead of using coins or bills, digital money is stored on computers and can be used to buy things online.

How Technology Changes Money

As technology changes, so does the way we handle money. Today, you can pay for things using your phone, buy stuff online, and even invest in companies with just a few clicks. In the future, who knows how money will work? The important thing is to stay curious and keep learning about it!

Saving for the Future

Even if money looks different in the future, the habit of **saving** will always be important. The sooner you start saving, the more prepared you'll be for whatever comes your way.

Activity: Imagine the Future of Money!

Draw a picture of what you think money will look like in the future. Will it still be coins and paper bills, or will everyone use digital money? What kind of cool technology will we use to pay for things?

CHAPTER 20 : YOU'RE A MONEY EXPERT NOW!

Congratulations! You've learned so much about saving, spending, and investing money. You've practiced setting goals, making smart money decisions, and even learned how to give back to others. Now you're ready to take on the world as a **Money Expert**!

What's Next?

Now that you know how to handle money like a pro, keep practicing. Save your money, invest wisely, and don't forget to have fun along the way. Remember, even small amounts of money can grow into something big over time!

Final Activity: Teach Someone Else!

You've learned a lot about money, so why not teach someone else? Talk to a friend or family member about what you've learned. You can even help them set their own money goals or start saving. Being a money expert means helping others too!

Conclusion: Keep Growing Your Money Skills
Money is something you'll deal with for the rest of your life, so keep learning and growing your skills. Whether you're saving for something small or planning for your future, always remember the lessons you've learned here. You've got what it takes to be a **Money Boss** for life!

CERTIFICATE OF MONEY MASTERY

This certifies that _____ **has successfully completed the Money Master program and is now an expert at saving, spending, and investing!**

Date: _____

Signed: _____

AFTERWORD

Writing Smart Money for Kids has been a journey of dedication and passion, and I couldn't have done it without the unwavering support of my family. I'd like to extend my deepest gratitude to my wife, whose patience, encouragement, and countless hours spent helping me bring this book to life have been invaluable. Her love and support kept me focused and inspired every step of the way.

To my wife and kids, thank you for being my motivation and for believing in the vision of this book. I hope that the lessons shared here inspire young readers and families to take positive steps toward financial freedom and a brighter future together.

ABOUT THE AUTHOR

S. Deep Perera

"About the Author

S. Perera is a dedicated author and parent of three child, who grew up in a modest family with big dreams. Through perseverance and careful money management, they transformed early financial struggles into a life of economic balance. With a passion for teaching kids the value of saving and smart investing, S.Deep Perera brings practical, kid-friendly guidance to families everywhere. Their journey from limited means to financial stability serves as a motivating foundation for readers to start their own financial journeys."

www.ingramcontent.com/pod-product-compliance
Lightning Source LLC
Chambersburg PA
CBHW040324220526
45473CB00009B/2562